Airbnb Business Blueprint

A Simple, Step-by-Step System to Turn Property into a Six-Figure Cash Cow

Josh Hall

Table of Contents

Introduction

If you have ever thought about running an Airbnb, you have come to the right place. It can seem very confusing and daunting to begin with, but if you have the right guidance, you can definitely do it. There is a reason why Airbnb has skyrocketed in popularity. People are able to connect with others who have properties available to rent for shorter periods of time. This means guests have more flexibility with the types of properties they stay in as well as pricing and experiences. As a host, you have the opportunity to create a business for yourself with whatever property you currently have. Airbnb has so many different options, including renting out single rooms, communal spaces, and entire properties. Whatever property you have on hand and whatever you're looking to invest in, you can definitely find a place for Airbnb rentals.

Throughout this book, we are going to go through a blueprint to help you get started with your Airbnb journey. You will gain information on everything—from discovering why you want to start running an Airbnb, to all of the tips and tricks you need to market and run your property well. This will result in happy customers having great experiences and will also result in you being able to increase your income.

Chapter 1

Why Start an Airbnb Business?

Starting an Airbnb business can be one of the greatest things you do for your finances and your own business journey. However, in order to set yourself up right, you need to understand the good and the bad that comes with it. This will allow you to have the entire picture in mind and not have unrealistic expectations. In this chapter, we are going to go through reasons why you should start an Airbnb business as well as the few negative aspects that you might need to consider.

Benefits of Running an Airbnb

There are tons of benefits to running your own Airbnb. It would be pretty much impossible to go through every single one of them, so we are going to go through a few of them that are the most prevalent. These are the ones that people typically mention as their reasons for starting the Airbnb business. It's also the reason they continue on with it because they enjoy the many different aspects of running an Airbnb. If you identify with any of these benefits, you are probably the right type of person to start an Airbnb business.

Time Flexibility

Most of us would agree that having more flexibility in our days is very necessary. We all want to have full control over our time so that we can do what we love as well as take care of our personal tasks. In fact, working from home is such a desired perk in any job, that people will take a salary cut in order to get it. This is not because people enjoy working from their bedrooms, but the fact that working from home gives you some sort of flexibility in your day. When you start an Airbnb business, you have this flexibility for yourself. You are in complete control of your time and can decide when and where you want to do things.

When you sign up to host on the Airbnb platform, you will be given a calendar where you can block out certain days you are not available. If you do not want to handle guests at a specific time, you really don't have to. The date you select will be completely off-limits to any guests and bookings. If you are looking to plan a vacation at any point, you can book those days out so you do not have to be at your Airbnb to take care of the guests. Perhaps you have your family or friends coming into town for a special event– you don't have to ask permission for that time off. Alternatively, you might find that your home is in need of some TLC and you want some time to take care of the issues and repairs. Blocking off these times will allow you the space to take care of your home and ensure that everything has been done right.

When you run your own Airbnb business you do not have to answer to anyone. Even if you don't have a traditional reason for not wanting to open your home to guests, you can do this at your discretion. This really helps you to plan your life around your own schedule instead of working with somebody else's. Time and flexibility are definitely two of the biggest perks that come with running your own Airbnb.

You Would Be In Full Control

Being in full control of your own life and your own business makes you feel powerful and like you have everything together. When you run your own Airbnb business you have full control over every aspect that surrounds it. Running an Airbnb means that you have control over the upkeep and design elements of your house. If you choose to be a more traditional landlord, you lose a lot of the control. This is because your tenants will be able to change things around in your property even if you don't particularly like it. Even though the home still technically belongs to you, practicality states that the home is your tenants. Since they are the ones that are living in it on a daily basis, you will not be able to check how they are taking care of the home or if they are making changes. Airbnb allows you to check in on your home at regular intervals when you are changing guests.

Another aspect of control is control over payments. The Airbnb platform requires the guest to pay before they stay and book at any home on the platform. The owner of the home will get paid and does not have to deal with the stress that many landlords have. Since everything is handled on the platform, there is no need to chase down guests or tenants for their money. You also have full control over how much you charge per night. This means that you can maximize your profits through various different factors. This helps you to increase the amount of money you make per month or per season.

You Get To Meet Different People

This one is definitely for all the extroverts out there. When you run your own Airbnb business, you'll be able to meet lots of different people. People from all over the world will be checking in to your Airbnb. It is basically like bringing the world to your doorstep. I have heard of so many people who have made lifelong friendships through Airbnb. You will find that guests are incredibly friendly, and because you are the expert in the area, they will want to come to you for guidance and assistance throughout their stay. Becoming a great host will allow you to get many return visitors throughout the duration of your Airbnb business.

This actually helps you to expand your knowledge of the world and what is going on in other countries. You get to learn more about what other people are going through and their experiences. Your eyes will be open to things you never would have experienced or knew about before. This is definitely one of the most interesting aspects of running an Airbnb. You will learn tales and stories about multiple people from different ethnicities, backgrounds, socioeconomic statuses, and various other differences. Gaining a new perspective from other people actually expands your insight and allows you to grasp more knowledge. You will find that it allows you to be more empathetic and more understanding of other people. This matters greatly in the world around us as well as in many professional standings. You will find that being exposed to multiple different people helps you to relate to various people you might meet in your everyday life. This might not seem like a traditional benefit from running a business, but it is definitely something that adds richness to your life. Eventually, even the most introverted airbnb host finds out how rewarding it can be to meet various different people from all over the world.

Risks That Come With It

Along with all the positive aspects that come with running your own business, there are also some negatives that you have to consider. It is important to note that many of these things can be managed through time, patience, and strategy. However, in certain cases, you will just have to deal with these negative aspects. Like any business, there will always be risks involved. It will be your job to ensure you're doing your part in order to mitigate the risks. This will give you a better chance of succeeding in your business.

You Might Get Unruly Guests

Unruly guests are definitely going to be a potential risk factor. You will likely not be able to meet your guests until they check in. At this point, it will be too late for you to do anything about it. Collecting a breakage deposit is always a good idea because if your guests were to break something or damage your property, you will have financial compensation for it. Airbnb also has insurance (AirCover) tied to it, so if you do put in a claim for damages, you will likely be fairly compensated. This being said, it is always a huge hassle if you do get guests that do not respect your property and end up damaging it.

Income Is Not Guaranteed

Like with many other businesses, income is typically not guaranteed. Rental properties usually have high seasons and low seasons. This means there are certain times of the year with lots of people looking to book with you and other times where it will be completely quiet. It is up to you to plan for the low seasons so you still have some finances to handle what needs to be done. Planning is definitely key when it comes to this, and there are definitely strategies you can put in place to make your property more attractive in the low seasons.

Clean Up and Upkeep Is Your Responsibility

There are not many people who actually enjoy cleaning up, but at the end of the day, if you own a rental property, it comes with the territory. You will need to make sure that your property is clean and maintained well so that every guest that comes in will have an excellent experience. Guests will be leaving reviews on the platform and getting negative reviews could deter future guests from booking with you. This is why you need to ensure that you are completely consistent with the type of experience you are giving each guest.

Chapter 2

Market Research Stage

Market research is an essential part of starting an Airbnb business. Doing this properly will help you to set yourself up in the right direction. You will have a better chance of attracting the right type of guests and increasing your profit margins. At the end of the day, your Airbnb is a business and you need to be making money from it.

Who Are Your Guests?

When you are trying to do market research you need to understand what your typical guest is going to look like. This is based on various factors. If you already have your property and are looking to rent it out, you will need to understand exactly what type of person would be staying in that area and in that type of home. For example, if you have a one bedroom apartment in the city, a large family is not going to be your target audience. However, singles or couples who are looking to travel and see the city would be drawn to this type of property. If you have a property in the business district of your city, business men and women would also be attracted to that area. You can then target your marketing approach based on the type of people you know will be staying at your property.

Realistically look at the type of property you have as well as the area it is situated in. Try to put yourself in the mindset of somebody who would book that property. You can also go onto Airbnb and find other properties similar to yours in a similar area. Have a look at how they market their properties and to who their target audience is. If you better understand your potential guests and how to market your property towards them, you will be more successful.

Understanding your potential guest is incredibly important because you need to cater to them. Different guests will have different needs. For example, business professionals who are always traveling will be looking for a place that is close to business centers and has access to Wi-Fi. These are the things that are most important to business professionals because they are looking to work. They might also need a designated workspace on the property so that they can take online meetings and have a place to concentrate on their work. This means you can purchase a desk and chairs and create a productive work environment for them. Since you know your target audience, you will be able to understand their needs and ensure that they have the best experience possible. This will result in more repeat guests as well as reviews that show similar guests that your property is the best for their needs.

Assess the Area

If you already have a property, there's probably not much you can do about the area it's situated in. In this case, understanding the type of guest is going to be the most important research you do. On the other hand, if you are looking to purchase a new property for your Airbnb business, you should definitely assess the area before you buy. The area in which your Airbnb is situated is arguably one of the biggest players in whether or not it is going to be successful. Certain locations are simply more lucrative than others. This is for various reasons but there are certain markers to look out for.

If you're looking to invest in a property for short term rentals and Airbnb, you need to look in cities that are quite popular for tourists or business travelers. They should have access to amenities as well as tourist attractions. A city that has a strong economy, great transportation services, nearby shopping centers, and various other amenities will be the best one to invest in.

When you are considering a specific city or area, it is a good idea to understand the high and low seasons. For example, certain cities or states will only be popular in the summer months. Understanding this will allow you to purchase the right property for you. You will also have realistic expectations on the booking potential of the property. Doing some research on the growth of the tourism sector in that city is essential. You would want a town or city that seems to be growing economically. This means you will have a better return on investment. If a specific city looks like it's on the decline, it is definitely not going to be a good investment, as you might end up struggling to advertise the home as well as find it very difficult to sell it if you need to down the line.

These days, it is actually pretty easy to find statistics for Airbnb's in certain cities or areas. All you need to do is type it into your internet search bar and you will get plenty of results that will help you out. Ensure you are cross referencing the data you are receiving, so that you fully understand how each city or state performs. This will help you better decide on which area is going to be the most beneficial to your Airbnb business.

Check Out the Competition

If you want to fully understand how much you could potentially be making in a certain area with a specific property you're looking to invest in, you will need to check out the competition. Luckily, the Airbnb platform makes this incredibly easy. All you have to do is sign in as a potential guest and research the properties in the area you are in. You will be able to see the types of properties that are available in your area and how much people are charging guests per night. This will allow you to see which properties are the most successful and you can decide on why this is. Perhaps there are certain amenities that are drawing guests in or it could be a specific type of property that is most successful in certain areas.

You will also get a good idea on how to competitively price your Airbnb in regards to the other ones in the area. This will help you to plan out your finances better and ensure that you are not over or under charging for your area. Researching your competitors will also allow you to find out if there are any gaps in the market. If you're able to offer something unique or something that makes your property more noticeable, you will likely attract more guests. It doesn't have to be anything massive; simply offering a small amenity or advantage will definitely attract more people to your property.

Setting up the Property

The great thing about running an Airbnb is that you can inject your own personality into the property. You can highlight the areas you love about your property so you have a unique space for your guests. Most guests understand that when they're staying in an Airbnb, it is someone's home. That "homey" touch makes it different from staying in a hotel, which can sometimes be too stiff and clinical. Never feel shy about adding a few personal items to the property.

If you are starting with a bare-bones property and you need to fill it with items, you should start with the basics. Think about the rooms that you have in the house and what each room would typically need. For example, the bedroom would need a comfortable bed, extra linen, storage, and a few decor pieces. You can make a list for each room so that when you go shopping, you know exactly what you need to purchase. Keep in mind your target guest and ensure you are filling the space with the things they would need. Not every guest will need every kind of furniture. You don't want to overspend on certain things that are simply unnecessary and will go unused in most cases.

Don't be afraid to move around the furniture and decor pieces in the home. The goal is to make it look as inviting as possible.

If it is possible to make the space look bigger by furniture placement, you should consider it. This part of the process is definitely trial and error, and it might take a while for you to discover what works and what doesn't work. You can always change it up as you figure out the better ways to do things.

During the setting up process, it is important to do general maintenance checks as well. You will need to make sure that the plumbing and electrical appliances all work well. It's not going to be a good look on you if your guests are the ones who figure out that things are not working the way they should. You should take some time to hire a professional to check that everything is going to run smoothly. This type of check will need to be done periodically, since general wear and tear will take place naturally.

Cleaning and Turning Over the Property

After every guest, you will need to turn over the property so it's ready for the next one. If you are really busy and have guests back to back, you will only have a few hours to turn over the property. Even if the time in between your guests is quite long, you should still try and clean the property as soon as possible. This is because during the cleaning process, you are also checking to see if there are any damages done to the property or the items in the property. You will need to report this as soon as possible in order to make an insurance claim and notify the guest.

The best thing you could do for the cleaning and turning over process is to create a checklist for yourself. This will help you to streamline everything and ensure that each guest gets the exact same experience. This will also help you to get to every area and ensure that you do not forget anything. Certain areas in the house will need more time and attention than others. Cleaning and restocking certain items should take place at the same time as this will make things go quicker and be more seamless for you.

The first thing you will need to do is to replace all towels and linens in the home. Even if guests have not used a specific area, you never truly know whether it's dirty or not. It is best to stay on the side of caution and clean out everything. Remove towels, bath sheets, bath mats, pillowcases, bedding, and tea towels. You can send them off to be washed and replace them with new ones. Ensure that you also leave a few extras for the guest to use if needed. Then you can move on to the kitchen, since this is likely going to be your biggest cleaning project. You will need to ensure all the dishes have been washed and put away in the correct places. If you have a dishwasher, this will need to be emptied. Have a look at all of the appliances and utensils to

ensure they are clean and functioning properly. Fridges, washing ·
machines, and storage cabinets need to be inspected and cleaned
out if necessary. You can then wipe down the kitchen surfaces,
taps and hardware, and take out the garbage.

Moving onto the bathroom, you will need to clean the toilets
and ensure they are spotless. The same goes for the sink, mirror,
and shower or bath tub. Have a look to see if anything has been
left behind from your previous guests and remove them. You
might need to restock things like toilet paper and toothpaste if
you do provide this to your guests. Double check the drain holes
so you know they are clean and not clogged. Then you can
empty the garbage cans and move on to the next room.

The rest of the house will be pretty simple since there aren't
many areas to clean. For entertainment areas, living spaces, and
the bedrooms, what you need to do is ensure that the floors and
furniture are wiped and cleaned. Make sure there isn't anything
left lying around and all surfaces that collect dust are dusted
well. You can then go ahead and restock any consumable items
your guests would need for the day. If you provide things like
condiments, salt, and feeding products, have these on hand to
provide guests when you are restocking.

During the cleaning process, you are going to be re-staging the
house. This means you need to revert to default settings.

Sometimes it can be confusing to do this, so one of the best strategies is to set up your house, take pictures, and use this as your guide every time you turnover the property. This way you can ensure that you are keeping the same standard and your guests can expect this standard each time they stay with you. The goal is to make sure that each guest feels like they are being welcomed and taken care of. Making an effort with cleaning can actually help you get amazing reviews. One of the biggest reasons people leave negative reviews is because the Airbnbs they have stayed at have just not been taken care of or cleaned properly. Since this is such an easy fix, make sure that you do not fall into the trap and end up getting bad reviews.

The House Rules

House rules will be the dos and don'ts for your guests when they stay at your property. These are incredibly important so your guests understand what is expected of them and there is no miscommunication between the both of you. It also helps them to evaluate whether your property is right for them. You will have the opportunity to set out your house rules on the Airbnb website. Guests can see it before they book so that they understand what will be expected of them in advance. You can also send them the house rules via email once they have completed their booking and confirmed they will be staying with you.

Simple Is Better

When it comes to writing out any kind of rules, simple is always going to be the best option. If the rules are too long and complicated, then your guests are likely not going to read it and will not stick to the rules. Using simple language is essential, especially if you get international guests. Not every guest staying in your home is going to be a native English speaker. If you use words that are too complicated, you risk losing the attention and understanding of these guests.

Since the rules are posted on the Airbnb platform, it is important to not overdo it. A common mistake is to write too many rules for your guests to follow. The issue with this is it turns off a potential guest from booking with you. At the end of the day, your guests want to have a relaxing stay at your house, and only being able to eat in one corner of the house is probably not what they are looking for.

Your house rules should probably only be around one page. This gives you enough space to write out your most important rules, and limits you so you don't go overboard. Ensure that you send your guests the house rules as well as leave a printed copy somewhere in the house so they can easily access it. A few common house rules are as follows:

- No smoking

- No noise after 10 PM

- Additional guests need to be cleared by the homeowner

- No pets

- Check in and check out times

Safety

Your house rules should also have some safety and security rules in them. This is to ensure that your guests are safe and your property is secured. These house rules can include closing and locking the doors and windows, as well as not lighting any candles, or things that can cause fires. You will likely have a few safety requirements of your own, so be sure to include them in your house rules so your guests are aware of them.

Some Cultural Rules

Every house, host, and country is completely different, so there will be some cultural elements that you might want to add. You can utilize your house rules as a way to educate your guests on specific cultural aspects that you expect from them when they stay in your home. For example, many households require that nobody wears shoes inside the home. If you come from a background like this and you require a guest to do the same, you should add these into the rules. You can even add a little explanation as to why things like this are done.

Emergency Details

Even if you have done your best to ensure that your guests will have a safe stay on your property, emergencies still happen. Ensure that your guests understand what to do in the case of an emergency. You can highlight where they could find a first aid kit or a fire extinguisher in your home. If there are any natural disasters or the area is prone to certain types of emergencies, notify them and leave a note of how to deal with the situation. You should also leave emergency contact details of the police, fire department, hospital, and your own contact details so that your guests can get in contact with the relevant people in the event of an emergency.

Chapter 4

Marketing Plan

Marketing is an essential part of running any kind of business. When it comes to Airbnb, you will be marketing your property on the Airbnb platform. The goal is to stand out from the rest of the properties so that you can get bookings consistently. One thing to note is that even the best marketing will never get you a 100% occupancy rate. This is incredibly unheard of and not something you should be aiming towards. In fact, anything above a 60% occupancy rate is great. This means that of all the listed times available for your property to be booked out, 60% of the time is filled. Having this kind of realistic expectation will allow you to be more successful in your Airbnb endeavors. Applying the tips and tricks we will be talking about in this chapter will aid you in getting high occupancy rates and making the most profit.

Taking Elite Photos

The only way people will know what your Airbnb looks like is through the photos you post on the Airbnb platform. Taking great photographs is one of the best ways to attract people to your property. You will find that the properties that have professional and clear photos are the ones who get the most bookings. There are many things that you can do to help people to live through the photos. You will notice that there are three pictures that show up first on any listing. These will be the most important photos. If you have any unique aspects to your property, you should upload pictures of these aspects to those slots. Perhaps you have an exceptionally large living space, a pool, or an amazing outdoor area. Anything that can grab the potential guests attention so they would be more likely to book with you.

The rest of the photos also have to reflect your property and frame it in the best light. You should have at least one or two photographs for every room or area in the house. People want to actually know what they are paying for when they book through the platform. Try and take your photos at a time of day where light is brightening up the room. Typically, early morning is one of the best times to take photos because the light isn't as harsh but it still brightens up everything. You could also try taking photos at golden hour, which is about an hour before sunset. It is best to use natural light rather than the artificial lights from lamps and indoor lighting. Natural light brings a brightness and a softer feeling to the space. It is also a good idea to shoot your photographs into the corner of a room rather than flat on. This will give the room dimension and make it seem bigger. Try taking a photo on a flat wall and then try aiming a camera into a corner to see the difference. You will quickly notice how much better shooting into a corner makes the photographs look. Try taking many different pictures from various angles so that you can get a better idea of what is working and what isn't.

Another option would be to hire a professional photographer to help you get the best quality photos. This is definitely an investment, but it is worth it if you are able to showcase your house in the best light possible and ensure you get the most bookings. You should never underestimate the power of photographs on the Airbnb platform. If you are unsure of the type of photos you should be taking, you can have a look at other listings and see the difference between the popular ones and the unpopular listings. This will give you a better idea of the photographs that are drawing people in.

SEO and Titles

SEO stands for search engine optimization. When you are able to use SEO you will allow potential guests to find your property a lot easier. When they type in keywords, they will be able to see your property first. The trick is to know what keywords to put into your listing. You can use SEO in the description or the title of your listing.

A great way to see whether or not you were using the right keywords is to do a search test and see where your listing falls on the page. If you are way down at the bottom, you are not using the right keywords in your description or title. If you are quite high up, then you can be sure that you are using the right words. You can look at the listings above yours to see what kind of words they are using that allows their listings to be more visible.

Descriptions

You want your description to pop off the page and attract as many people as possible. Even though your title is incredibly important, your description is what's going to carry on peeking your guests' interest. Your description doesn't have to be very long–as long as it is effective. Whatever you described in your description box needs to reflect in the photos that you have uploaded. Take some time to scroll through your photos and see if you can bring them to life using words.

You should also consider structuring out your description so it's easy for the reader to go through. Using multiple paragraphs with shorter sentences is typically a good idea. You do not need to put every piece of information in your description. All that needs to be there are the most important things. You need to use words that bring life to your property and avoid words that are too generic. If you have a word in mind, you can use a thesaurus to find alternatives that could bring more meaning and visualization to the words on the page. It is also a good idea to speak directly to your target audience and show off the aspects of your property that are going to be beneficial to them. Have a look at a few other properties' descriptions to find out how they've structured them and get some ideas for yourself as well.

Getting Reviews

Getting good reviews is going to be essential when it comes to running an Airbnb. The more positive reviews you have, the more people will want to book for you. There will be a sense of credibility that is tied to your property when there are multiple reviews being left. The first thing you need to do is make sure your customers are all satisfied. If the guests that stay in your property are happy with the service and the experience they've had, they will be more likely to leave a good review. The entire experience will start from the time they have booked until the time they check out. This means you have to communicate with them throughout the process and ensure you are building a good relationship with your guests. This helps them to feel like you really care about them and they will be far more likely to leave a positive review.

If there ever is a problem that pops up, you need to be on the ball. Most people aren't upset by issues that arise, but they will be if they are not being heard. Ensure that you are doing your best to resolve any concerns or issues your guests might be facing. I can almost guarantee you that even if there is some sort of negative experience, your guests are not going to remember if you handled it well enough.

Once your guest checks out, you can send them a check out message that requests some feedback from them. Requesting feedback is a bit more low key than asking for a positive review on the Airbnb platform. It will also help you to get better in the future and know exactly what your guests are looking for.

Another great way to prompt your guests to leave you a review is to review them. Airbnb allows both the host and the guest to review each other. Once you send out your review to them, they will only be able to see this review if they leave one for you or they have to wait over two weeks. Out of sheer curiosity, a guest will more likely than not review the host so they would be able to see the review left of them.

Chapter 5

Financial Plan

Working on your finances is incredibly important with any kind of business. You need to have a plan set in place so you do not overspend unnecessarily. Having a financial plan helps to maximize your profit and ensure you are purchasing the right items as well as funneling your money into the correct areas. You'll be able to plan better and understand how much money to raise.

Expenses

Understanding what your expenses are will allow you to create a budget that is realistic. The amount of money you spend on your expenses will be tied directly to how much profit you make. Knowing all the costs will allow you to set a reasonable nightly rate so you are not charging too little and ending up making very little profit. It is important to track all of your expenses throughout the duration of your business. Many of your expenses could change over time and that means you would need to adjust your nightly rate accordingly.

Mortgage

Your biggest expense is going to be your mortgage payment. This will differ depending on the type of property you have. Some people choose to run Airbnb's on the same property they live on, but in a separate room or a smaller property that is on the larger one. Ensure you are only taking out a mortgage that you can afford.

Insurance

It is essential for you to take out a separate insurance for your property, because you don't want to be liable for a large sum of money if guests are injured on the property or if something happens and needs to be replaced or fixed. There are many property insurance plans that target short term rentals. You should get one that covers you in this regard. Traditional property insurance isn't going to cover you if your guest gets injured on the property or if you are sued for some reason. Do your research so you can get the best deal. In many cases property insurance is lumped in with your monthly mortgage payment, which makes it a lot easier to pay.

Utilities

Utilities such as electricity, water, waste removal, gas, and internet will need to come out of your Airbnb revenue. This will likely be the second biggest expense after your mortgage payments. You can expect to pay around 20 to 25% of your monthly costs towards the utilities.

Maintenance and Cleaning

Every property needs to be well-maintained, and this is especially so when you're renting it out to other people. Things like lawn care, plumbing, and electrical appliances will all need to be considered when doing your maintenance. If you are doing maintenance yourself, this will be a lot cheaper. However, it does take away time from you. If you're looking to hire a landscaper or a gardener to take care of your lawn, you need to add this into your budget. The same goes for any plumbing or electrical maintenance.

Cleaning costs can also be considered home maintenance. You can definitely pay somebody to do the cleaning and turn over your home, but you need to ensure they are doing it properly and to your liking. Giving clear instructions to the people who are doing this is essential. It is also important to note that professional cleaning will come at a cost, so you do need to add this to your budget.

Furnishing

All Airbnb's need to be furnished well so your guests have everything they need when they're staying with you. In most cases, furnishing will be a one time expense unless something breaks and needs to be replaced. It is a good idea to purchase good quality items so they last longer and are more durable. Have a look at what you need in your Airbnb and budget for them in your financial plan.

General Supplies

Your guests would need basic items such as coffee, trashbags, soap, and toilet paper. There are probably many other disposable things that you would like to purchase for your guests and all of these need to be in your budget. Many Airbnb hosts love to create a welcome package for the guests because it adds a personal element to the home. In fact, guests who receive a personalized welcome pack tend to leave better reviews because they feel as though the host has taken the time to really consider them and their needs. You can buy these items in bulk to reduce the amount of money you will be spending on them.

Fees

There are a few different kinds of fees that can be associated with running your own short term rental or Airbnb. When you advertise your property on a short term rental website such as Airbnb, the platform will take fees from the host. All sites will be doing this differently, so you do need to research and find out what the fees will be. Fees could also differ depending on your area. These fees are typically taken out of your nightly rate when somebody books with you. This means you need to ensure you're accounting for the fees when you set the rate on the platform.

Depending on the city or state your Airbnb is in, there might be homeowners association fees and registration fees that need to be paid. Many neighborhoods have a homeowners association that will only allow short term rentals if you are part of the association. This means that there are yearly fees that need to be included in your expenses. Registration fees are when your city decides that every short-term rental needs to register with them. This is becoming more and more common, so be sure you're doing your research so you are not skipping out on this as this could result in penalties.

Taxes

Nobody likes to pay taxes, but unfortunately it is a part of living in a society. There are a few taxes that you will have to consider when you are running your own Airbnb. The truth is, Airbnb has become a major threat to the hotel and rental industry. Because of this, there have been many legalities put in place for Airbnb owners. It is important for you to contact your government offices to find out what taxes you will be liable for. You will likely need to pay traditional property taxes as well as taxes on the income you are making. The amount of taxes you will be liable for will depend on the city or state you are in.

CHAPTER 6

Automating and Scaling

As your business grows, it's going to be increasingly difficult for you to handle everything on your own. While you might have been able to do the multiple tasks that come with running an Airbnb when you only had one property, adding two or three properties to your business is going to complicate things. Once you learn how to automate your processes, you will be able to scale your business a lot quicker. Things will become a lot easier for you to handle and you will have a lot more free time to do other things.

Automated Messaging Systems

Guest communication is incredibly important, but it can also be very time consuming. If you have multiple properties and various guests that are constantly checking in and out, it can be so difficult to stay on track with all the communication. Missing out on the communication can leave guests feeling as though you do not care about them, and this can lead to bad reviews. You want to be able to provide your guests with the best experience possible, but you also don't want to be sitting by your computer answering the same questions over and over again.

As a general rule, you should be sending messages to your guests before, during, and after their visit to your Airbnb. You should also be replying to their queries and concerns promptly. One of the best ways you can do this is to have email templates ready to go. If you use an Airbnb automation tool such as "Host Tools", you will have access to templates that will be sent out to your guests at the appropriate times. If you do not want to sign up for tools like this, you can type out generic messages and copy and paste them into the emails as needed. However, this is likely more time consuming than getting a program to do it for you. Here are some of the instances in which you can create message templates:

- Booking confirmations

- Booking inquiries

- Booking requests

- Check in messaging

- A check up message

- Check out message

- Message to leave a review

Check-in and Key Exchanges

Meeting your guests upon check in is doable when you have one or two properties, but as you scale up your business, it's just not going to be feasible. Automation makes it a lot easier for your guests to seamlessly check in and check out of your Airbnb without you needing to be there. Many Airbnb hosts will sign up with a property management company that will do all of this for them. There will be somebody there to help check in and check out the guests, and you have to just pay the fee to the property management company. This is an incredibly convenient way to do things.

Another option is to install smart locks in your Airbnb. When you do this, it is not required for a person to be physically present to handover the keys to the guests. The entries will be keyless and that makes it very secure and convenient. Your guests will receive a unique access code that will expire after they check out. This kind of system is actually way more secure than regular keys because the keys can be copied. If you have a guest that is looking to steal or access the home without your permission, they will not be able to do so when there is a smart lock installed. You do not have to replace locks, replace lost or broken keys, or need to rescue a guest who has accidentally locked themselves inside or outside the home. You'll be able to control everything remotely and it makes the whole process a lot more seamless and less stressful for everybody involved.

If you do not like the idea of the smart lock, there are other options. You can consider getting a lock box or key safe where you place the keys for your guests to pick up. Your guests can then drop off the keys in the same box when it is time for check out. You still do not have to be there while they're checking in and checking out. This is also a cheaper option if you are looking for automation on a budget.

Cleaning Services

Cleaning your Airbnb's is going to take quite a lot of time if you have to do so every time your guests check out. If you hire a professional property management company, they won't be able to handle all of this for you. You should also look into getting a reliable cleaning provider who will come in and clean as needed. It is usually best to go through a company rather than an individual. If an individual cleaner gets sick or is unable to make it to your property when your guests check out, is it going to cause a huge problem for you. When you hire a company, you can rest assured that someone will always be there to clean up and take care of your home. It is definitely a costly option, but you have peace of mind and there will be a higher standard of cleanliness.

Pricing Automation

When you have a short term rental, your pricing strategies need to change all the time. In the high seasons, you can get away with charging more because your property is going to be in more demand. In the low seasons, you can drop your prices so you can still attract people to the home. Pricing strategies can also change from weekdays to weekends. Since weekends tend to be more in demand, you will be able to charge more on these dates. On top of that, you might want to offer some discounts to guests who want to stay for longer periods of time. Having a dynamic pricing strategy is essential to making the most amount of profit through your Airbnb.

You can utilize pricing tools from external sources or use Airbnbs smart pricing data to help you. This will change your pricing based on the data that is provided through researching surrounding properties that offer similar services. You do not have to do anything besides input a few preferences and basic data. After that, it is all up to the software. The program will automatically increase and decrease the prices when necessary.

Chapter 7

Faqs and Tips

There is truly a lot of information to take in when you are on the way to becoming an Airbnb host. There are also many tips and tricks that you could implement to help make the process easier and ensure that you and your guests are getting the best experience possible. In this chapter, we are going to go through all of these.

Frequently Asked Questions for Hosts

How do you become a host?

The process to become an Airbnb host is pretty easy. All you need to do is sign up on the Airbnb platform and follow the various prompts. The process is simple to complete and everything you need is going to be on the website. You will need to create an account as well as fill in all the relevant information.

Airbnb does not regulate who signs up as a host on the platform, so there won't be somebody coming to check in on your property. Just make sure you create a listing that is attractive, so you can have the best chance of getting bookings.

What is a Super host?

A super host is a regular Airbnb host that has been identified on the platform to provide excellent service. These will have to be experienced hosts who get extraordinary reviews from their guests. Once you reach the super host status, you will be awarded a badge so guests can be notified of this. There will also be a super host filter, and you will likely be able to charge more as one. There are various requirements to be a super host, including: completing 10 trips or three reservations with a total of 100 nights booked, having a 90% response rate, having less than a one percent cancellation rate, and having an overall rating of 4.8 that is maintained consistently.

What is AirCover?

This is simply reimbursement coverage that Airbnb offers to the host. As soon as you sign up as a host, this is automatically applied to you and it is completely free. The host will qualify for up to $1 million in damages and liabilities in the case of issues caused by a guest. With this being said, it is simply not enough to have this type of insurance and you should look into getting your own outside insurance.

What are the cancellation policies like?

There are actually various cancellation policies that you could pick depending on your needs. You can pick a flexible, strict, super strict 30 days, or super strict 60 day policy for your Airbnb. You will have to bear in mind that very strict cancellation policies are a bit of a turn off to many guests and this could lead to getting fewer bookings. You can find out more about the different cancellation policies on the Airbnb website. These can change every now and then, so it is important to stay up-to-date with new information surrounding it.

Tips and Tricks

Create a theme

An Airbnb is supposed to create an experience for the customer. When your guests check in, they should feel like they are on holiday or that the space serves their needs. When you have a theme, everything is cohesive and flows nicely and naturally. It can also help the guests get into the mood of the surrounding area. Your themes can be based on the city or type of location your property is situated in. For example, if you have a beach cottage, you could fill your home with coastal themed furniture and decor pieces. If you have a city apartment, modern and clean finishes might work best.

Give your guests some guidance

As mentioned earlier, giving a guest a welcome package is a great idea. The welcome package can be used as an opportunity to introduce the guests to various places and items they could enjoy in the city, state, or area your property is located in. If you want to get the best reviews, you should do your best to ensure that your guests are having a great time overall. Giving them a list of suggested restaurants, activities, and places to visit is a great way to add a personal touch to your property.

Never oversell your property

One of the biggest mistakes people make when they list properties is they oversell it. They make it seem so amazing and get the guests' expectations too high. The mentality behind this is to attract as many guests as possible. However, it actually has a negative effect on your reviews and the guests' experience. If the guest expects to stay in a five star resort and is met with a three star cottage, they are going to be very upset. The ratings will be incredibly low and it will hurt your potential future customers. This is why it's so important to be honest. In fact, it is better to undersell your property slightly, so that you are able to exceed your guests expectations.

You set the expectations that your guests have. You either need to meet them exactly or exceed them. This is the only way you will be able to get the best reviews and ensure that your guests have the best time and experience while they're with you. At the end of the day, even if you have an amazing listing, negative comments and reviews can really bring it down and you will end up losing a lot of credibility.

Consider your neighbors

Even though your neighbors do not pay you any money or are not involved in the Airbnb process, your relationship with them really does matter. Your neighbors could end up complaining and make it very difficult for you to continue with your Airbnb business if they are upset. They could also interrupt your guests' stay for various reasons. This is why you should speak to your neighbors as often as possible and give them whatever relevant information they need. If they are aware that you will be running an Airbnb, they will be a lot more forgiving and can prepare themselves accordingly. You should also ensure you have notified your guests to be mindful of the neighbors so they do not overdo it with noise and disruptions.

Start cheap

When you are first starting out with Airbnb, you aren't going to have any reviews and this means your credibility is quite low. The only thing people have to go on is your listing. A great way to attract more people to your listing is to make your nightly rates cheap. People will be more willing to book at cheaper rates, and you can get a good amount of people to stay at your property. The first few months should not be focused on profit, but rather on getting the word out there and setting yourself up for the future. Once you have built up your business and have a good customer base, as well as some good reviews, you can increase the price to a reasonable rate that makes a profit. You will have reviews that show other guests how amazing the experience was and it will be easier to attract more people to your property.

Conclusion

Running an Airbnb business is one of the most rewarding but also one of the hardest things you're ever going to do. There are tons of new skills that you will need to gain, as well as learning to be flexible and planning properly. As time goes on, you will definitely see what works for you and what doesn't. Even though this is an Airbnb blueprint, every person will run the Airbnb slightly differently. You can learn from other people and their stories, as well as from your own trial and error. You should always be open to learning more about the business so that you can continue to grow with it. There's always new tactics, strategies, and information coming out, so this book is just the starting point. A successful business is one that is continuously growing and changing to play towards the target audience and the market.

You can definitely find success with Airbnb if you are willing to put in the work. The first few months are going to be a lot of hard work because you will be finding your feet. After that, things will start to get a lot easier because you will understand the process and you can start automating. This is when you'll really start to see the fruits of your labor and you will likely enjoy it a lot more. Running an Airbnb helps you to meet so many new people, have great experiences, and increase your income so that you can increase your standard of living.

References

Benefits of being an airbnb host. (2014, October 6). LearnBNB.com - Hosting Advice, Tips, & Resources. https://learnbnb.com/benefits-airbnb-host/

Comprehensive list of airbnb host expenses. (2020, December 1). Unbound Investor. https://www.unboundinvestor.com/comprehensive-list-of-airbnb-host-expenses/#:~:text=When%20you%20run%20a%20short%20term%20rental%20you

Fernández, A. (2022, February 23). *How to write up an airbnb business plan: Free PDF template*. Vacation Rental Owners & Property Managers Blog - Lodgify. https://www.lodgify.com/blog/airbnb-business-plan/

Hosting tips for airbnb: 17 expert tricks to be a superhost. (2020, February 26). Robemart Blog. https://robemart.com/blog/hosting-tips-airbnb-superhost/

How to automate your airbnb rental & increase efficiency. (2020, July 3). Host Tools. https://hosttools.com/blog/short-term-rental-automation/automating-airbnb-rental/

Karani, A. (2019, August 7). *The 4 steps of airbnb market research*. Investment Property Tips | Mashvisor Real Estate Blog. https://www.mashvisor.com/blog/steps-airbnb-market-research/

Lavinsky, D. (2021, December 26). *Airbnb business plan template [updated 2022]*. Growthink. https://www.growthink.com/businessplan/help-center/airbnb-business-plan

Making a hosting business plan. (2021, June 7). Airbnb. https://www.airbnb.co.za/resources/hosting-homes/a/making-a-hosting-business-plan-98?locale=en&_set_bev_on_new_domain=1667307748_NWMy YzAzMzZhODI4

Pros and cons of starting an Airbnb. (n.d.). Www.seeff.com. Retrieved October 31, 2022, from https://www.seeff.com/news/pros-and-cons-of-starting-an-airbnb/

The airbnb cleaning checklist: A step by step guide. (2022, April 18). Like Cleaning Services Group. https://likecleaning.com.au/the-airbnb-cleaning-checklist-a-step-by-step-guide/#:~:text=1%20Here%20is%20a%20checklist%20for%20c leaning%20Airbnb

Walls, P. (2022, September 15). *40 pros & cons of starting an airbnb host (2022) - starter story*. Starterstory. https://www.starterstory.com/ideas/airbnb-host/pros-and-cons

Wong, A. (2022, April 28). *How to get more bookings on airbnb (& attract more guests)*. Alex Wong Copywriting. https://alexwongcopywriting.com/how-to-get-more-bookings-airbnb/

Writing helpful house rules. (2021, May 13). Airbnb. https://www.airbnb.co.za/resources/hosting-homes/a/writing-helpful-house-rules-21?locale=en&_set_bev_on_new_domain=1667307748_NWMy YzAzMzZhODI4

www.ingramcontent.com/pod-product-compliance
Lightning Source LLC
Chambersburg PA
CBHW030534210326
41597CB00014B/1146